Contents

Chapter 1
Blast-Off

I was reading Grandad's Amazing Space Journal in my room. It was a kind of diary full of facts. The wall-screen came on. It was Grandad. He smiled at me from the screen.

"I've done it, Billy!" he said.

I jumped up from my chair. "You have? You've really done it?"

Grandad grinned. He looked happy, with his wild grey hair like a mad professor and his big smile.

"I've got the Falcon Mark II spaceship running. I was thinking ..." He stopped and looked at me.

"Yes?" I asked. My heart was beating like a drum.

"I was thinking, Billy, that you might like to test fly it with me?"

I was so excited that I couldn't say a word. I just nodded.

"Good," Grandad said. "Meet me at the spaceship junk yard in five minutes."

"I'm on my way!"

The screen went blank. I ran from my room and grabbed my jacket. Mum was in the hall.

"Billy," Mum said, "where are you going?"

"Over to Grandad's," I said.

"I don't want him taking you up in one of his old spaceships!" she said.

"Don't you trust him?" I asked.

"Billy ... it's not that I don't trust him. It's just that when he was still working as an astronaut he had a crash in space."

"He never told me," I said.

Mum shook her head. "Perhaps you should ask him about it," she said. "And remember – no spaceships, OK?"

But I was already running out of the house.

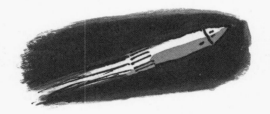

Grandad was my hero.

He had been an astronaut for many years, but now he ran a spaceship junk yard. It was a great place, full of bits of old spaceships, fins and wings and huge engines.

There were whole spaceships in the junk
yard too. I loved to climb inside these, strap
myself into the pilot seat and pretend I was
flying through space.

I ran through the junk yard, past piles
of twisted metal and the nose cones of old
starships. It made me excited to think that all
this scrap metal around me had once travelled
through space on exciting trips to planets and
far away stars.

Grandad was the first person to set foot on Mars, back in 2035. That was 40 years ago, but now Grandad was too old to be an astronaut.

A few years ago he bought the junk yard, so that he could be near the spaceships he loved so much. He liked to build them from all the bits in the junk yard. Last year he mended a huge one, and took me for a short flight around the world. Grandad also wrote a big journal full of amazing facts about the solar system. I was always reading it! I thought about what Mum had told me. Grandad had never said anything about a crash. Was that why he stopped being an astronaut?

The spaceship was silver and shaped like the head of an arrow.

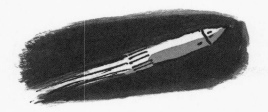

"Welcome aboard the Falcon!" Grandad said, poking his head through the sliding door and waving at me.

I ran up the ramp and into the ship and stared around me in amazement.

"It's fantastic!" I said. Two seats had been placed in front of a large view-screen. There were more seats behind, like in a bus, with view-screens all round the side.

"It used to be a tourist ship, Billy," Grandad told me. "In the old days it took people on trips around the Solar System, flying close to all the planets."

"Can we do that?" I cried.

"No," Grandad said. "We're just going on a quick orbit of the Earth, to make sure the ship

9

works. Strap yourself in the co-pilot's seat and we'll blast off."

I sank into the seat and strapped myself in.

I wondered if I should ask him about the crash, but decided to leave it till later.

Grandad sat in the pilot's seat and ran his hands over the control panel.

"Hold tight, Billy! We're taking off!"

I was pushed back in my seat as the Falcon roared and shot into the air like a bullet.

Chapter 2
Mercury

I looked through a side screen at the ground. I could see the city getting smaller and smaller. The streets looked like a map. We had to go fast to escape the Earth's gravity, which tried to pull us back.

Grandad said, "We're leaving planet Earth behind us, Billy, and heading off into space. My word, this does bring back memories!"

Soon the Earth was a small ball below us. Grandad tapped the control panel.

He was frowning.

I said, "What's wrong?"

"Strange," he said. "The controls aren't working properly."

We were heading *away* from Earth, instead of going round it. It was getting smaller and smaller.

A loud voice cried, "EMERGENCY! EMERGENCY!"

"What was that?" I said.

"The ship's computer," Grandad said. "Something's going very wrong."

I gripped the arms of my seat and stared through the view-screen. All I could see was black space – and then, in front of us, the distant sun.

"We're heading for the *sun!*" I whispered.

Grandad was still trying to work the controls. He was pressing button after button, and looking worried. Sweat ran down his face. Nothing was happening. We were still heading towards the sun.

"EMERGENCY! EMERGENCY!"

Grandad said, "Computer, why aren't the controls responding to my commands?"

The computer said, "OVERRIDE! OVERRIDE!"

"What does that mean?" I asked.

"It means that the original computer that was in the tour ship has taken over," Grandad said.

Suddenly I heard a sound behind me. "Ladies and gentlemen," said a voice. "Welcome to Solar System Tours – we hope you enjoy your trip around the Solar System!"

I spun round in my seat.

A man in a blue uniform was standing behind us. He was talking to the empty seats around him. He looked like a shimmering ghost – I could see right through him!

"It's a holographic tour guide!" Grandad said.

"You mean, it isn't really a man?" I asked. "And anyway, what does holographic mean?"

"It's a kind of image made from light," said Grandad.

He stood up, reached out, and passed a hand through the ghostly guide.

"But we're still heading towards the sun!" I cried.

The holographic guide said, "Wrong, Space Ace."

"My name's Billy!" I said.

"We're heading towards Mercury," said the guide.

Grandad said, "Billy, it looks like you got what you wanted – we're going on a tour of the Solar System!"

The guide said, "You're right, sir! And I'm your guide. I'll talk you though your tour of all the planets in Sol's System. (Sol is the name of our sun, by the way.) And if you have any questions, any at all, please ask!"

"Great!" I said.

"To our right," said the holographic guide, "you can see the planet Mercury. It is the second smallest planet in the Solar System, and it has no atmosphere round it – no air or gases of any kind. It is 58 million kilometres from the sun."

I stared out at the tiny grey planet, covered with thousands of round crater holes.

"Mercury," said our guide, "moves around the sun very fast. This means that it has the shortest year of any planet, just 88 Earth days long. During the night, it's very cold – 180° centigrade below zero. But during the day it's hot – around 430° centigrade. It would be impossible for human life to exist on Mercury."

I watched the small grey ball as we looped around the planet and flew away.

"And now we are heading towards the second planet out from the sun," said our guide. "Venus."

Chapter 3
Venus

Grandad turned to the ghostly tour guide.

"How long will we be in space?" he asked.

"The tour will take just two days," said the guide. "We will be travelling at top speed all the way."

The guide stepped forward and pointed through the view-screen. "In front of us, ladies and gentlemen, you can see the planet Venus, which is 108 million kilometres from the sun."

The planet soon filled the view-screen. It was covered with what looked like pale yellow clouds.

"Venus is the closest planet to Earth," said the guide. "But it is even hotter than Mercury. This is because clouds made from carbon dioxide trap heat on the surface and don't let it escape. The surface temperature is 480° centigrade. That is more than four times hotter than boiling water! In 1975, a Russian unmanned space probe, Venera 9, landed on Venus and sent back pictures for nearly an hour before it burned up. These pictures showed a surface of sharp rocks and huge stones."

We sped away from Venus and I watched the planet get smaller and smaller.

"Now we will soon pass planet Earth," said the guide, "but I won't say anything about this planet because I think you know all about it already! After Earth, we will fly close to Mars."

Mars ... I thought. I glanced at Grandad. He was staring through the view-screen. I wondered if he was thinking about the planet which he had visited more than 40 years ago.

Chapter 4
Mars

We passed Earth, a round ball covered with blue seas and bright white cloud.

Grandad said, "I'll try and get in touch with your mum. She'll want to know where you've got to."

He reached for the two-way radio, but I said, "No, don't!"

He looked at me. "Billy, what is it?"

I looked away. "It's only ... you see, Mum didn't want me to go into space with you," I whispered. "She said something about a crash."

Grandad put an arm round me. "Billy," he said, "I've never told you before. I *was* in a crash. It was my fault ..."

I stared at him. His eyes had a far away look. "We were on our way back from Saturn. We were just coming through the asteroid belt. I was piloting, and ... Well, I crashed the ship into a spinning asteroid. I wasn't thinking fast enough and I lost control. It was my fault ..." He stopped, then said, "One man died. I hurt myself quite badly. That was the last trip I did. The truth was, the Space Agency didn't want me, after the crash."

He turned away and stared through the view-screen. I didn't know what to say. I just reached out and held his hand.

One hour later I looked through the view-screen at the Red Planet – Mars.

The guide said, "In the year 2035, Commander William Jones was the first person to set foot on Mars."

I glanced at Grandad. I could see tears in his eyes as he stared down at the red planet.

"It seems just like yesterday," he whispered.

The guide said, "Mars is—"

"Please," said Grandad, "I'll tell Billy all about Mars, if you don't mind."

The guide bowed and fell silent.

Grandad said, "Mars is smaller than Earth, Billy, and is 228 million kilometres from the sun. It's very cold on the surface of the planet. When my team and I were there, the temperature could be anything between minus 27° centigrade and minus 133°. You would freeze to death if you didn't wear a space-suit to protect you!"

He smiled and shook his head. "Some scientists thought that life might exist on Mars. We looked everywhere, and made experiments, but we didn't find anything. Many millions of years ago, there might have been life. But Mars has been slowly moving away from the sun, getting a little colder all the time."

I stared down at the craters, and the long lines scored across the face of the planet, which looked like canals.

"We landed near Olympus Mons," Grandad said. "It's a huge, dead volcano 26 kilometres high! There, you can see it!"

He pointed, and I could see a big circle, dark red against the pinkish sands of Mars.

"And there," Grandad said, pointing through the view-screen, "are the two moons of Mars, Phobos and Deimos."

I watched them spin past the ship. They looked like knobbly potatoes. "Phobos is 27 kilometres long," Grandad said. "Deimos is slightly smaller, just 15 kilometres at its

longest point. They're getting closer to Mars, and one day they'll crash into its surface."

The ship turned, and headed away from the red planet. Grandad reached out and gripped my hand.

"In a short while," said the tour guide, "get ready for the fantastic sight of Jupiter!"

Chapter 5
Jupiter

Three hours later Grandad pointed through the view-screen.

"That's amazing!" I cried out.

"Jupiter!" said the guide. "It is about 778 million kilometres from the sun, and it's the biggest planet in the Solar System."

Not only was it the biggest – it was also the most colourful. It was covered with stripes of cloud – orange and brown and yellow.

"Jupiter is what is called a gas giant," said the guide. "You cannot see the surface of the planet. It has a rocky core about the size of Earth, but this is covered by a layer of liquid metallic hydrogen 33,000 kilometres thick. On top of this is a covering of liquid non-metallic hydrogen 22,000 kilometres thick, and then a thin atmosphere of hydrogen and helium gas, just 1,000 kilometres thick."

"There's the red spot!" I said, pointing to Jupiter. I was very excited.

Jupiter was famous for its huge red spot.

"The red spot is really a storm," the guide told us. "It has been raging round Jupiter for hundreds of years. The spot is 40 thousand kilometres long and 11 thousand kilometres wide."

We flew closer to Jupiter, so that it filled the entire view-screen.

"This is as close as we can come to the planet," the guide said. "Jupiter throws out a lot of radiation, which is dangerous to human beings."

"Look," Grandad said, "the moons."

We were flying next to two big moons, and I could see other moons in the distance, all circling around giant Jupiter.

"Jupiter has more than 60 moons. Ganymede is the biggest moon in the Solar System, even bigger than the planets of Mercury and Pluto. Scientists think that a long time ago, some of the moons might have been planets like Earth and Mars, but they were captured by Jupiter's strong gravity, and now they circle the gas giant for ever."

I looked at the guide. "Have we sent any unmanned rockets to Jupiter?"

"In the 1970s, Pioneer 10 and 11 flew past the planet, and they sent back the first close-up pictures of Jupiter and its moons."

Through the view-screen I saw a faint ring system. I pointed. "I didn't know Jupiter had rings!" I said.

The guide grinned. "In 1979, the Voyager 1 probe discovered a system of rings made up of millions of tiny grains of dust."

"Could we live on the moons?" I asked.

"Perhaps on the outer moons," the guide said. "But even then we would have to live in special domes to protect us from Jupiter's strong radiation."

I stared at the planet as we moved slowly away. "Goodbye, Jupiter," I whispered. "Goodbye, red spot!"

Chapter 6
Saturn

"Saturn is the second biggest planet in the Solar System," the guide said. "And do you know why it is famous?"

"Because of its rings!" I said.

"Correct."

I thought that Saturn was the most lovely thing I had ever seen. The big light brown planet filled the view-screen. Around the middle of the planet was the famous ring system. Each ring was a different colour, silver and gold and black, all shining in the light of the planet.

"Saturn is another gas giant," said the guide. "Like Jupiter, it has a rocky core. And like Jupiter it has a layer of liquid metallic hydrogen but it's thinner, about 15,000 kilometres thick. Above this is another layer – this time of liquid non-metallic hydrogen which is 25,000 kilometres thick. On top of all this is a thin atmosphere of hydrogen and helium gases."

The guide pointed through the view-screen. "Saturn has more moons than any other planet. Do you know how many moons it's got, Space Ace?"

"My name is Billy!" I said. "And I think it has more than 30 moons that we know of."

"That's right! Scientists think that perhaps it once had many more, but they smashed into each other and shattered into millions of bits of rock. These tiny bits of rock formed into the rings we can see today."

"How far away is Saturn from the sun?" I asked.

The guide smiled and said, "It is 1.4 billion kilometres away."

1.4 billion kilometres! I thought. I looked through the rear view-screen. Our sun was a tiny shining star in the distance.

Grandad was staring out at Saturn. "My very last mission was to Saturn," he said. He looked sad.

I decided not to ask him about it.

Chapter 7
Uranus

It was another three hours before we reached the next planet – Uranus.

We were now even further away from home.

The guide said, "Uranus is 2.9 billion kilometres away from the sun. It is smaller than Saturn and has an atmosphere of hydrogen, helium, and methane – which means that no human being could breathe on it! Like

Jupiter and Saturn, Uranus is also a gas giant. Also, like Saturn, it has a ring system."

Uranus was not as lovely as Saturn. It was pale blue-green, and its rings were faint and tilted towards us.

I pointed. "Is that a moon?"

"Correct, Space Ace!"

I was getting mad by then. "My name," I said, "is not Space Ace! I'm Billy!"

From the corner of my eye I saw that Grandad was laughing. "Once we're back on Earth, I'll have to fix the computer program," he said.

The guide was saying, "Uranus has more than 25 moons. The largest is Titania."

We raced past Uranus.

"And now for Neptune!"

Chapter 8
Neptune

"Now we are 4.5 billion kilometres away from the sun, and in front of us you can see the planet Neptune."

I thought about all those kilometres. Every day I walked a kilometre to school – and Neptune was 4.5 *billion* kilometres from the sun ...

I felt dizzy thinking about it!

Neptune was the same size as Uranus, and had 4 rings. It was a bright blue colour and hazy. It looked cold.

"Like Uranus," the guide said, "the atmosphere of Neptune is made up of hydrogen, helium and methane. The weather on Neptune is perhaps the oddest thing about the planet. Storms last for hundred of years, and blow at over 600 kilometres per hour! Just try to hold onto your umbrella in that!"

I looked over at Grandad, who whispered, "I think he's trying to be funny!"

"Does Neptune have any moons?" I asked.

"It has 13 known moons," said the guide. "The biggest is Triton, and it is famous for being the coldest known object in the Solar System – its surface is 235° centigrade below zero."

We flew around the planet, and minutes later the guide said, "If you look to your left, you will see Triton."

We raced past a great brown ball. We were so close that I thought for a second that we were going to hit it.

"There is another interesting fact about Triton," the guide said. "Scientists predict that, in less than 100 million years, Triton will come so close to Neptune that it will be torn up into millions of tiny pieces. It might even form a ring system like Saturn's."

I thought about that, and all the other facts the guide had told me. What a story I would be able to write on Monday, when my teacher asked the class about what we did at the weekend!

"And now the tour of the Solar System is almost over. The last stop is Pluto."

Chapter 9
Pluto

We were out on the very edge of the Solar System now, nearly six billion kilometres from the sun.

"People used to think that Pluto was the ninth planet from the sun, but now they say it's not a proper planet but a 'dwarf planet'," the guide said. "Scientists think that once, a very long time ago, it may have been a moon of Neptune, and that it smashed into another moon and was pushed out to the very edge of the Solar System, like a snooker ball."

We were getting close to Pluto. It was tiny and round and made of ice, like a bright blue snowball.

"Pluto's surface temperature is around 225° centigrade below zero. It is made up of frozen methane, which is why it is blue. It takes more than 248 years to go round the sun."

We shot round Pluto in a huge loop.

"If you look through the view-screen to your left, you will see Charon. This is Pluto's only moon, and is about half the size of Pluto."

We raced away from Pluto and its moon and off towards the sun, which was a tiny twinkling star in the distance.

"And now we begin the long flight home," the guide said. "We will reach Earth in just under one day. However, there is one more thing to see before then."

I thought about that. What hadn't we seen so far on our trip around the Solar System?

"The asteroids!" I said.

Chapter 10
Asteroids, and Home

"Let's get some sleep," Grandad said. "The guide will wake us when we reach the asteroid belt."

We pulled two bunk beds from the wall and lay down. I couldn't sleep, though. My head was full of all the fantastic sights I'd seen.

I must have fallen asleep at last, because I was awoken by the computer calling, "EMERGENCY! EMERGENCY!"

"What's happening?" Grandad said, climbing from his bunk.

We ran to our seats and strapped ourselves in.

I stared through the view-screen and gasped.

We were in the middle of the asteroid belt!

The guide said, "The asteroid belt lies between Mars and Jupiter."

"Please, guide," Grandad said, "shut up!"

But of course the guide took no notice.

"Asteroids can be as small as a house or as big as a few hundred kilometres across. They are made of rock and metal."

The ship was flying itself through the asteroids, which tumbled past us like a torrent of falling stones. I thought we were going to crash into one at any second.

I looked at Grandad. He was staring with wide eyes through the view-screen. I wondered if he was remembering the crash, all those years ago.

"There are more than 50 thousand asteroids in the belt," the guide went on.

I really didn't want to know that! It seemed that every one of them was trying to smash into us.

At that second, we did hit something. The ship shook and clanged like a bell.

"EMERGENCY! AUTOMATIC STEERING DAMAGED. THE PILOT MUST TAKE OVER AND FLY ON MANUAL!"

Grandad looked over at me. "That means I've got to get us through the asteroids myself, without the help of the computer."

I held onto my seat while Grandad pressed buttons and tapped at the control panel. His hands moved in a blur, as he plotted our course through the tumbling asteroids.

I covered my eyes when a big rock loomed up at us – but the smash never came.

I opened my eyes. We were still racing through the asteroid belt. Big rocks rushed towards us, but Grandad steered the ship out of the way again and again.

I held onto my seat as we swerved this way and that. It was like being on the fastest roller-coaster in the world.

I stared at Grandad as he pressed buttons and switches. He looked fearful and excited at the same time.

Then a huge rock loomed up in front of us.

"Hold on tight, Billy!" Grandad yelled.

I gripped the arms of my seat and shouted in fear. The rock filled the view-screen, but at the very last second Grandad pulled the ship up and away from the asteroid.

"Done it!" he said.

Seconds later he was steering us through the last of the asteroids, and he was smiling like I'd never seen him smile before.

His cheeks were wet with tears.

Minutes later Grandad sat back in his seat and said, "I've done it, Billy. I've done it. We're safe."

Through the screen I saw that we had
passed through the asteroid belt. Clear space
lay ahead of us, and in the distance I made out
the small, blue shape of planet Earth.

I was crying too. I flung myself at Grandad and hugged him.

Two hours later we were back in the junk yard.

Grandad brought us down between the piles of scrap metal and old starships.

We sat in silence for a while, and then I said, "Grandad, that was the best weekend I've ever had in all my life!"

He smiled and shook his head. "I never thought I'd get us past the asteroids ..."

I had a sudden idea. "Perhaps," I said, "we could go back one day and this time land on Mars."

"That would be really exciting," Grandad said. "But first I've got to get you back home in time for Sunday dinner."

We climbed down from the ship and left the junk yard. I looked up into the night sky.

"Grandad," I said, "I've just thought of something."

"What?" he said.

I pointed up at the full moon. "The guide never told us about *our* moon!"

Grandad laughed. "Then I'll tell you all about it," he said.

As we walked hand in hand through the city, Grandad said, "The moon is the only satellite of planet Earth, and it is a little over 384 thousand kilometres away from Earth. It has no air and no life. In 1969, Neil Armstrong was the first person to walk on the moon, Space Ace!"

Laughing, we hurried home.

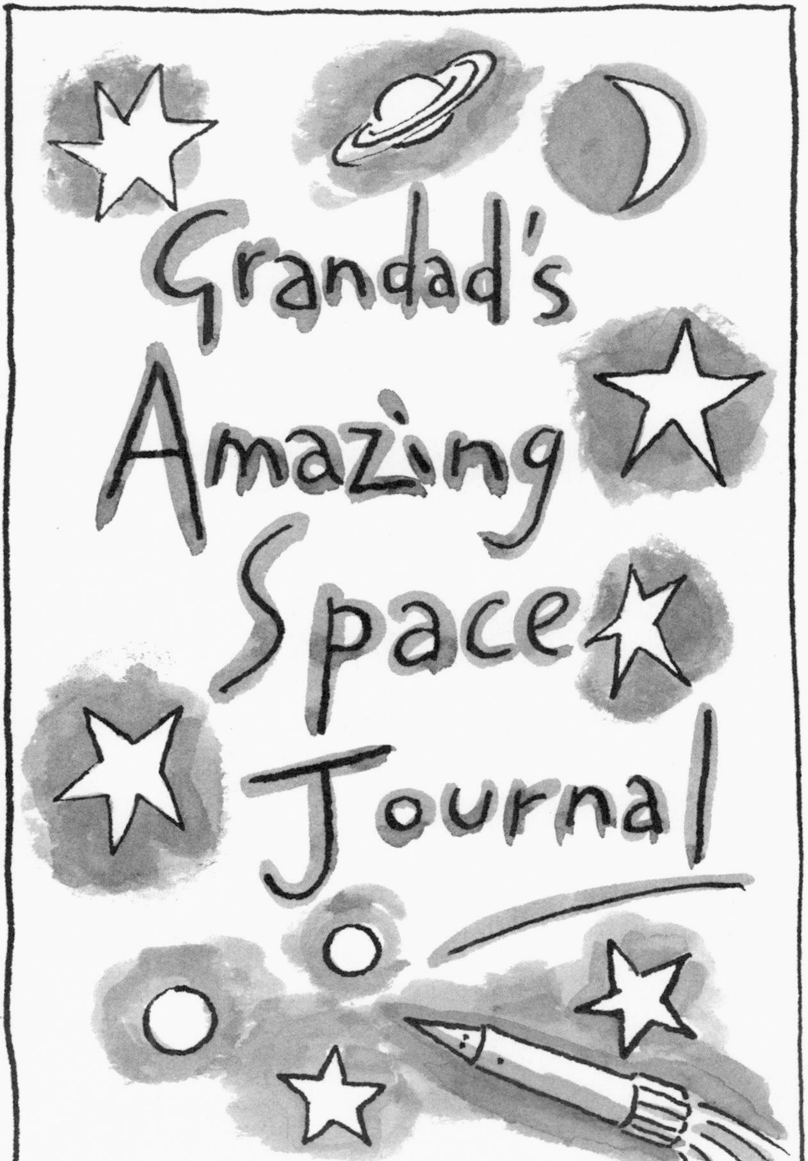
Grandad's
Amazing
Space
Journal

SIZZLING FACTS about the Sun!

1. The sun is five billion years old and almost 150 million kilometres from Earth

2. The temperature at the core of the sun is 15 million Kelvin

3. In five billion years' time, the sun will swell into a huge red ball. It will grow 150 times bigger than it is now, and shine a thousand times brighter

Miraculous facts about Mercury!

1. Mercury is the second smallest planet in the Solar System, and it is the closest planet to the sun

2. Mercury is named after the Roman messenger of the gods

3. The planet has no moons

Feed Graham the Martian Gerbil before the next space flight

GD

Fantastic facts about Venus!

1. A year on Venus (the time it takes the planet to move around the sun) lasts for 224 Earth days

2. Venus is yellow because of all the sulphuric acid in the atmosphere. This may come from active volcanoes

3. Venus has no moons

4. Venus is named after the Greek goddess of love and beauty

Forty years ago Today I walked on Mars GD

Marvellous Facts about Mars!

1. Mars takes 687 Earth days to move around the sun - so a year on Mars is much longer than an Earth year!

2. Mars is named after the Roman god of war

3. The atmosphere on Mars is made up of lots of different gases, carbon dioxide, nitrogen, argon, and tiny amounts of oxygen, carbon monoxide and water vapour. It is thin and deadly to human beings!

Jubilant facts about Jupiter!

1. Jupiter moves slowly around the sun, so that a year lasts for 12 Earth years

2. It spins very quickly, so that a day lasts for almost ten hours

3. The cloud-top temperature is minus 150° centigrade

4. Jupiter is named after the ruler of the Roman gods

Fabulous Facts about Saturn!

1. A year on Saturn lasts for almost 30 Earth years

2. A day (the time Saturn takes to spin on its axis) lasts for just ten Earth hours

3. The cloud-top temperature is minus 180° centigrade

4. Saturn is named after the Roman god of farming and the harvest

Remember Billy's birthday present – he likes Luna Chocs!
G.D.

Ultimate facts about Uranus!

1. Uranus is named after the Greek god of the heavens

2. It was discovered in 1781 by William Herschel

3. The cloud-top temperature is minus 220° centigrade

4. Uranus is four times larger than Earth, and it is the third largest planet in the Solar System

Nifty facts about Neptune.

1. Neptune is named after the Roman god of the sea

2. It was discovered in the 1840s by John Couch Adams, Urbain Leverrier, and Johann Gottfried Galle

3. A day lasts for just over 19 Earth hours

4. Neptune is the fourth largest planet in the Solar System

Tomorrow.
meet Space Joe
at the Pluto
Pub for a
pint of
Jupitor Juice!
G.D.

Four Facts about *Pluto!*

1. Pluto spins slowly on its axis, so that a day on Pluto lasts for six Earth days

2. Its atmosphere is made up of methane. There may be nitrogen too

3. Pluto is named after the Roman god of the underworld and darkness

4. The planet was discovered by Clyde Tombaugh in 1930

Buy a pair of space socks! You can wear them all week and they won't smell! G.D.

Famous People in Space!

1. The Russian cosmonaut Yuri Gagarin was the first person to go into space when he flew right round the Earth in 1961

2. In 1962 John H. Glenn was the first American astronaut to fly around the Earth

3. In 1963 Valentine Tereshkova was the first woman in space

4. In 1965 the Russian Alexei Leonov was the first person to walk in space

Our books are tested
for children and young people by
children and young people.

Thanks to everyone who consulted on
a manuscript for their time and effort in
helping us to make our books better
for our readers.